Life After Loss

FINDING HOPE AGAIN IN GOD

by
Pam Dressler

Harrison House
Tulsa, Oklahoma

10 09 08 07 06 05   10 9 8 7 6 5 4 3 2 1

Life After Loss: Finding Hope Again in God
ISBN 1-57794-747-9
Copyright © 2005 by Pam Dressler
e-mail: findinghope@sympatico.ca

Published by Harrison House, Inc.
P.O. Box 35035
Tulsa, Oklahoma 74153

Contents

Introduction:
From Tragedy to Testimony

"Some friends are here to see you."

Those words changed my life forever. My youngest child, my three-year-old baby girl, my Alexandra Joy, had been killed. Nothing, absolutely nothing, could have prepared me for that news or for the horror of it all and the loss that I felt.

My prayer is that through the telling of my story and by showing how the Lord walked me through the days, weeks, and months after that terrible event, as He does still, you will be encouraged and changed as you see this example of God's character and glory shining brilliantly in the midst of life's difficulties.

Maybe you lost a child too. Maybe you lost a spouse, or a parent, or a very close friend. I want my experience—my responses, my family's walk through it with God in the midst—to give you hope when hope seems lost, direction where there is confusion, compassion where there is pain, encouragement where there is sorrow, the Word of Life—Jesus—where there is death. As you read my story, perhaps you will recognize it as yours as well.

1

The Questions

At her young age, Alli was starting to gain a measure of independence, and the night she was killed was no different. Even after being gently corrected at the beginning of a midweek church service, she still somehow managed to walk out of the church building never to be seen alive again. Alex was killed instantly when a freight train running on an unprotected nearby track hit her. The moment of impact, she was with Jesus.

I was not present before or immediately following the accident. Police officers, along with my pastor, came to tell me of the accident at work. Afterward, they took me to the church. Looking back, I remember that so many thoughts ran through my mind…

"Had I been there, she would not have died."

"Did I do something that caused this to happen?"

"Why didn't God miraculously keep her safe from harm?"

"Why didn't God bring her back to life when those who found her prayed over her and spoke life back into her body?"

"How is it possible that her purpose on earth is fulfilled at age three?"

"Why did God allow her to die?"

Even now I cannot answer all those questions, and I've come up with many more since that absolutely horrible night. However, I know the One who does have those answers, and I believe I can know the truth, perhaps not in my time but in God's time. As Christians, as religious folk, as born-again believers, it is very easy to spiritualize death. But the plain fact is that however we choose to explain it away and practically force ourselves and others to almost ignore the issue, death has a very real impact and is emotionally painful to all it touches. When your loss is as great as that of the death of your child, the impact shatters your heart.

Looking Forward

As human beings, it is natural for us to demand to know the cause or reason for just about everything. Never is this more evident than when we experience loss and death. Irrationally, we tend to place blame on the doorstep of Heaven. There is no doubt whatsoever that it was the enemy, Satan, who was responsible for the death of my baby, *not* the Lord. God didn't "call her home" or "need another angel." Satan is out to steal, kill, and destroy,[1] and he will stop at absolutely nothing to wreak havoc everywhere, especially among the Church and believers.

But "...thanks be unto God, which always causeth us to triumph in Christ...."[2] Praise God, we have power over the devil!

It has been a long, hard road to come to a place of looking ahead and not back. Reliving the horror and terror is always just at the edge of my consciousness. With hardly any effort, I can go back to that place of receiving the news and experience the first impact of the loss. I see the scene and the sequence of events that followed begin to play out in my mind, then again I see them start to replay, running over and over as if I'm watching the most terrifying horror film I've ever seen again and again.

Obviously, it isn't a good idea to revisit the past, but when it sneaks up on me, I make a conscious choice not to go there. When I am at a funeral, for example, I have to work very hard at controlling my thoughts so that I will not react to the reminder as if Alli's death just happened.

Those of us who have already experienced a deep loss know what it's like to appear on the outside to be functioning well but who are, in reality, only going through the motions. Once we reach a point of embracing God in the midst of our pain and begin receiving all that He wants to give us to help us through it, our desire to live again, to actively participate in life, starts to return. And I found that once I started living again, I had to intentionally keep on living so I wouldn't fall back into my previous state.

2

Looking for Answers

The Lord spoke to me in my spirit a few months after Alli's death to show me that if I try to apply everything I know and learn in order to understand "what happened back there," I will not find answers. Instead I will find confusion, condemnation, and guilt. I found myself writing, "LOOK FORWARD NOT BACKWARD," in my Bible, in notebooks, on bookmarks, everywhere. Writing this down didn't mean that I didn't have to continue making a conscious choice to look forward minute by minute, hour by hour, and day by day. It was a habit I needed to develop in order to steer clear of the confusion, guilt, and condemnation that always threatened to break in and shatter my peace of mind.

This brings me to a couple of important points to share with you regarding grief. Grief is a legitimate human emotion. The Bible does not tell us that as Christians we are not to grieve. It tells us we are not to grieve as the world grieves— without hope.[3] The Bible also says in 2 Corinthians 7:10 (AMP):

> **For godly grief and the pain God is permitted to direct,produce a repentance that leads and contributes to salvation and deliverance from evil, and it never brings regret; but worldly grief (the hopeless sorrow that is characteristic of the pagan world) is deadly [breeding and ending in death].**

Grieving is grieving whether you are a Christian or not. Jesus even experienced grief during His time on earth, probably more frequently than we do today. The Bible does tell us that He wept at the tomb of Lazarus.[4]

Grief can manifest in both physiological and psychological ways. I do not intend to talk about the different stages of grief; that is not my purpose. There is, however, a myriad of physical symptoms that you may experience, and it is good to know that grief is most likely the source. They will diminish over time and generally do not reflect a more serious health issue.

You may also experience difficulty in focusing your mind, in remembering simple things, and in maintaining your line of thinking. Of course, the Lord can and will help you conquer all of these problems should you experience them, but I just want to reassure you that physical and mental symptoms of grief do exist and will generally fade as time goes on.

A word about resources: There are a lot of different books, articles, and other material available for people who are going through grief. Of course, the Bible is the ultimate authority on life for the believer, and I caution you to measure everything you read against the Word of God. However, don't avoid secular publications simply because they are secular. Like the old saying goes, "Chew the hay and spit out the sticks." Many resources in the "secular" world are actually helpful to the Christian who has never before experienced a loss. Knowing generally what to expect does help. You may think the effect of a great loss you've experienced will be different for you, but don't expect it to be. I can't tell you how many times while reading a book on grief and loss that I said to myself, "Hey, that's me!"

There is, of course, an obvious emotional impact of grief. Anyone who has ever experienced a deep loss in life will attest that grieving doesn't stop after the third day. In fact, it isn't until a few months later that walking through the grief becomes the hardest. Following an overwhelming tragedy, the world around you doesn't take long to return to normal. Just look at what has happened in the Western world since the catastrophic events of September 11, 2001. The all-night prayer meetings, the candlelight vigils have all but stopped since the Twin Towers were destroyed. Let's face it, most people eventually stop praying for you, and you are left to your own devices to deal with the loss while staying connected with the Lord. To "get over it" is neither a rational nor, honestly, a possible thing to do.

I want to encourage you to face your thoughts, feelings, and emotions as much as possible, to work through all you need to in order to arrive at a place of peace and acceptance. Shutting down your emotions, hiding from life, or self-medicating will only prolong the pain you will necessarily go through in coming to terms with death. This attempt to escape from the cycle of grief I liken to the Israelites wandering in the wilderness: You will have to cover the same ground again and again until you deal with your feelings, thoughts, and emotions.

This doesn't mean you need to analyze every single second of your life from this point forward, but you do need to recognize which feelings and thoughts are still stemming from the grief process. Some thoughts you will recognize as just plain wrong. Those thoughts you cast down according to the Word.

Casting down imaginations, and every high thing that exalteth itself against the knowledge of God, and bringing into captivity every thought to the obedience of Christ.

2 Corinthians 10:5

Why Am I Mad at God?

It is not unusual to question the Lord. (He already knows what you are really thinking anyway!) You might even be angry with Him, but to be completely honest, that anger is misplaced. You and I do not have a right to be angry with Him. As children and servants of God, we can lay claim to all the rights He gives us, but holding on to anger and bitterness isn't one of them. I spent some time believing I had the right to be mad at the world because this horrible thing had happened to me. In fact, I was completely astonished that the world could keep on functioning normally—that, everywhere, people continued living as before— when my life and world had been shaken and abruptly changed by this absolutely horrible event that had happened to me. How dare they!

Anger and bitterness were trying to destroy me. I was only causing myself more problems by hanging on to them, and the truth of the matter is that I had no right to be bitter. If you do not resolve your feelings, you will begin to take that anger out on the whole world. Bitterness and anger do not lead to peace. You cannot permanently leave unfinished those angry conversations with the Lord nor can you allow bitterness, anger, or any other negative emotion to take control of your life.

I would be lying to you if I led you to believe that I didn't blame the Lord on occasion. I spent a couple of months wandering in the wilderness of sin and rebellion, and I knew it. I was angry and cynical. I wanted nothing to do with my family and friends. Even though outwardly I presented myself as being a good, strong Christian, I withdrew. I remember one particularly interesting Sunday morning in church. I had worked myself up into quite a state. We were singing songs like "God Is Good" and "Jesus Is Alive." My mental comments to the Lord went something like this:

"Oh yeah, You're so, so good. Alli is dead, but *You* are so good!"

"Jesus is alive, that's wonderful. Alli isn't, but as long as Jesus is, that's just great!"

To top it off, it was Communion Sunday and Pastor had a lot to say about the blood of Jesus and protection. Listening to his message succeeded only in making me more hysterical, and I insisted that we leave church early. My husband tried to get me out of my bad mood, but I would have none of it. I told him that he needed to leave me to my bad day so that there would not be bad weeks or months. Even in my hysteria, I recognized that I needed to go through a bad day here and there.

I kept telling myself that it didn't matter that I was self-destructing, but God wouldn't leave me alone. It took the harsh but honest words of a close friend for me to realize that I was not only hurting myself, but my family and friends as well. They had enough to handle already without having to deal with my bitter and angry attitude.

A Turning Point

The friend who spoke with me was a very close friend before Alli's death, but also during the time of the loss and after—a very faithful friend—someone I would listen to, someone who could "get away" with speaking to me so directly. I would have dismissed almost anyone else who had attempted to straighten me out by speaking to me in such a manner. It is important to note that not just anyone can step in, speak the truth, and really be heard by those of us who are grieving. At that point in my grief journey I made a personal decision that I would deal with my thoughts and feelings as they came and try very hard not to take out on anyone else the way I felt.

I realized that instead of stuffing my emotions away, piling up the hurt, and wandering around and around in my grief, I needed to reach out to God in my pain instead of pushing Him away. I slowly began to change my focus to seeing that perhaps by going through this dreadful experience (not that I had a choice!) in the right way—by drawing on God—I could somehow, in some way, help others in a similar situation.

In the next few pages I walk you through the details immediately following Alli's death for a couple of reasons. If only to encourage you through giving you a glimpse into an understanding of the horror, grief, and emotions I felt—to take that extra moment to hug your children a little bit longer and tell them you love them just one more time, or to take the extra moment to show your love to your other loved ones—the telling of my story and your reading it in the midst of your loss will be worthwhile. But also from my example, I want you to be encouraged to see the way God wants to shine His glory into your most adverse circumstances and learn more about Him from the way He revealed Himself to me during this time.

I especially want the ones reading my experience to understand the importance of maintaining a close, connected relationship with the Lord in order to be prepared *before* really needing it, whether the challenge is small or the circumstance severe. If, as a result of reading this book, you spend more time in the Word, expect God's glory to shine into even your darkest circumstances, and love your kids and those close to you more, then this book has accomplished much.

3

*Family, Friends, and the Church:
The Blessing of Fellowship*

The night of the accident I was working my first (and last!) night of a new part-time job at a hotel. What happened next was like something right out of a movie. Another staff member was sent up to the sixth floor to get me. Coming down in the elevator, I noticed there were two police cars in front of the hotel. (The elevator was at the back of the lobby and had a glass window that allowed its occupants to see into the lobby as well as out the front of the building.)

I remember wondering aloud if the police cars had anything to do with why I was being called to the manager's office. My coworker calmly replied, "Should they?" and being that I wasn't a law-breaker, I quickly answered, "No!"

In retrospect, that exchange aided in keeping me calm. In fact, up until the very moment that the police officer uttered those awful words that Alli had been killed by a train, I honestly did not have a clue that anything was even wrong. Now, you would think that seeing two police officers and your pastor (who was supposed to be at church) in your workplace would set off some alarms, but I can only believe it was the grace of God protecting my mind and my emotions. God's grace is truly amazing!

Naturally, I was very upset, crying when they broke the news to me. The hotel where I had begun working was in a neighboring city, so I had to be taken back to the church. Before we went too far, I started calling people on a borrowed cell phone, people I needed and people needing to know. Again, God is so gracious! I am gifted in the area of administration and just naturally went into what I call "crisis mode." I had to do things to stay in control. The Lord doesn't bless us with giftings simply for use in the employment world or for use in the church: He gives us gifts for us to use to help ourselves also, and those gifts can help us in every situation.

While the Lord was working on me, He was also working on the behalf of Oliver and the kids through the entire time. I am sharing with you the grim details of what Oliver walked through so that you can see the Lord's hand on every aspect of this experience. The Lord was with us from the beginning: He didn't come on the scene *after* the accident; He was there and is here all the time.

When Alli couldn't be found, the small church building was searched thoroughly in short order. It didn't take long to realize that Alli had somehow left the church. A call was made to 911, and the members started looking in the neighborhood. Honestly, how far could a three-year-old go in a matter of minutes?

Oliver and one of the pastors searched the overgrown lot next to the church up to a portion of fencing. The railway track lay beyond that but was not in plain sight from there. The train's whistle blew, but that was not a cause for concern at the time as it was a normal occurrence. Oliver noticed that the train had stopped, but he didn't give that a second thought either. The search continued and the Lord repeatedly said to him, "She's all right. She's with Me." Not knowing she had been killed, Oliver just figured that the Lord was protecting her.

A member of the church thought of going up on a nearby bridge to get a better view of the area, and that was when she was discovered. It was clear that she had not survived the impact of the train. The Lord had begun preparing Oliver by impressing on him that Alli was all right and blanketed Oliver with peace that Alli was safe in the arms of Jesus.

The other children, at this point, were in the church. It fell to Oliver to tell them that their sister had gone to heaven. They all cried, but since they understood that she was with Jesus, they were not overwhelmed with loss. You see, our children had always, always been involved in church and the things of God, and they didn't know any other reality than that of Jesus. They returned to the children's room to play while everything else was taking place. When I arrived, they came out to see and talk with me.

The unity of the Spirit of the Lord in believers and in families is another precious and helpful gift the Lord gives us. My first words—and indeed the reassurances that I gave to Jake, Krysti, and Glori when I first spoke with them—were almost word for word what my husband had told them before I arrived. There was so much strength in our family that night due to the unity of the Spirit we shared. I tell you those things that we spoke to our children (and ourselves) that night to show how important it is not only to stay connected as a family during a tragedy, but also to have an eternal focus.

I truly believe that we helped our children immeasurably through much of the work of grief by speaking to them what the Lord put in our hearts and mouths. We told the kids three main things:

1) Alli was *safe* with Jesus in Heaven

2) we will all see her again pretty soon

3) it is okay to cry and be sad.

These three statements are a reality to our children, and they accept these truths. These principles also kept us focused and out of debilitating grief, and we were able to share them with others, thus ministering a measure of peace to them also. God is so good!

You may have heard it before, but I want to reiterate that children usually understand things much better than we give them credit for. Sometimes they can more readily deal with the unfortunate issues of life than we adults who aren't always ready to cope with those things ourselves. I was so amazed at the kids' understanding.

I'll never forget the afternoon a few weeks after Alli's death when Jake, Krysti, and Glori were watching a Christian video, Gospel Bill, on sickness and healing. One of the main characters had gotten hurt to the point that death was a distinct possibility. As a result, one of the other characters was praying and believing God for her friend's healing and restoration. (Just to let you know, the character in question did receive healing by the end of the program.) The principles shared in the video struck a chord in my children, and afterward they discussed it among themselves.

They voiced their understanding that, just like the character in the video, Alli was too young to die and that she shouldn't have died, according to different promises in the Bible. Yet despite this seeming contradiction, they knew she was safe in Heaven with Jesus. They also thought that maybe God could send her back to us, but I think deep down they knew that wouldn't happen. With these things settled in their minds, off they went on some other childhood adventure. As I listened to this conversation, I was praying only that they would not ask me about what they had seen on the video. (I had not yet worked through those issues myself!)

Having faithfully attended an active and growing church and previously an even larger, active, growing church, there were honestly thousands of people across the country praying for us during the time surrounding the funeral. I want to encourage you that when you pray for someone, you can be assured that the Lord does move! We felt the prayers of our brothers and sisters literally, like a blanket on our shoulders. In fact, that blanket of prayer kept us on an even keel emotionally. It kept us going through the weeks following her death and through what could have been really difficult days. Do not underestimate the power of prayer!

> **And let us consider one another to provoke unto love and to good works: Not forsaking the assembling of ourselves together, as the manner of some is; but exhorting one another: and so much the more, as ye see the day approaching.**
>
> **Hebrews 10:24,25**

As well as the prayer cover we experienced, the Word of God that had been imparted to us by many well-known, anointed men and women on a consistent basis proved to be another amazing gift. When you sit in church for years and open your spirit to receive the Word, know that it is in you when you need it. Of course, it is important to read the Word yourself, but it is also extremely important to be in a Bible-believing church where Jesus is uplifted and preached consistently. Never could I have anticipated my daughter's death, but I know without a doubt that when I needed the Lord to sustain and strengthen me, His Word in me was what kept me in that place.

Starting to put the Word in you after the fact, after the loss, will help in the future, but it really isn't going to help very much in the present circumstance. Just as with the prayers of the saints, the Word that had been deposited in my spirit over the years kept me in a level of peace during this worst storm of my life. I cannot urge others enough to be in and stay under the mighty Word of God as much as possible.

It is important that even if you don't want to do it, do it anyway until the desire to do it catches up with you. Pray until you *want* to pray; read your Bible until you *want* to read your Bible; go to church until you *want* to go to church. Don't do it for someone else's sake either; do it for *you*, because you may need the Word and the Body of Christ someday!

Wherefore let him that thinketh he standeth take heed lest he fall. There hath no temptation

**taken you but such as is common to man: but
God is faithful, who will not suffer you to be
tempted above that ye are able; but will with
the temptation also make a way to escape,
that ye may be able to bear it.**

1 Corinthians 10:12,13

Praise be to God! The Lord knows so well our
limits in what we can deal with. My husband was
present on the scene initially and I was not. I
needed that time for the Lord to get hold of me
for me to gain some measure of control before
seeing my husband and children.

For Oliver, needing time to regain control of
his emotions was never an issue. I learned something very important, especially for a person
going through a great loss to understand: Even
though the Lord says we will not be tempted or
tested beyond what we can bear, *we can bear much
more than we think!* If you had asked me that
morning if I believed that I would be able to bear
the death of my child, I would have said
absolutely no way! Our God, though, knows us
better than we sometimes know ourselves.

The Bible says that Jesus has gone through everything that we have gone through and will ever go through.

For we have not an high priest which cannot be touched with the feeling of our infirmities; but was in all points tempted like as we are, yet without sin.

Hebrews 4:15

It is true that because Jesus did not have any natural children, one might think that He never had to bear the loss of a child. Jesus Himself did not, but His Father did. God lost His only Son to the most hideous and horrible death anyone could ever experience. God spoke to my heart shortly after Alli died and reminded me that He knew exactly how I felt because His child suffered death also. I was struck with how profound that is! We seldom meditate upon the thought of *the* Father as *a* father feeling fatherly emotions, especially in regard to the death of Jesus. He is truly touched with the feelings of our pain because He experienced it too.

4

A Funeral and a Burial

There isn't a chapter in the New Testament entitled "Funerals and Burials," but we can get the right idea by understanding what we are. We are a spirit, we have a soul, and we live in a body. When we die, it is our body that ceases to be (for a time, anyway). Our spirit lives forever. This is a fact we well understood and held on to in regard to Alli. Her body died, but her spirit was immediately received into Heaven.

Having never experienced death in such an intimate way before, the whole ordeal of a funeral and burial was new to us. Of course we had attended funerals, but other than the death of a close friend a few years earlier, we had never attended a Christian funeral. Nor had we been responsible for one…until now.

The Lord walked us through the entire process. Decisions we had to make that were too hard for me one day I found I could deal with the next. For example, we needed to go to the funeral home the morning after Alli was killed in order to pick out a casket and make arrangements for the service. Initially, I felt I could not do that. I sent my dad along with Oliver. It turned out that Alli's body had not yet been released from the hospital to the funeral home. We needed to wait until that happened before we could make those decisions. During that first afternoon, the Lord brought me to a level of peace so that I was able to take my place with Oliver the next day and tend to the details.

Making these arrangements was difficult, as you can imagine, but I was able to get through it. And with three other young children, it was necessary to explain what was happening so that they could understand. Having to explain the process to them actually helped us put the events into proper perspective.

If I thought going to the funeral home was hard, making the arrangements at the cemetery almost did me in. I didn't like the place at all. Unlike the people at the funeral home who were really great, compassionate, caring people, the "salesman" at the cemetery we dealt with rubbed me the wrong way entirely. I did not find him helpful, and I could not wait to get out of there. I found reading the literature to be very difficult, especially about markers and suggestions of what to put on them. Phrases like "too small, too sudden, too soon" brought my raw grief to the surface. Once I wrote the check, I ran out of the building.

I felt so agitated there, I asked the Lord why. I sensed the answer was that at a cemetery there is no Spirit of life, only death.

Although at the time I would have preferred to avoid both, a funeral and burial were necessary, but not just because that is what is traditionally done. To the world, a funeral or a memorial service is a chance to say goodbye and also to remember or celebrate the person's life. It is that, but it is more.

It is "that" because the service is also the point of acknowledging the finality of the relationship on earth. We remember our loved ones' accomplishments, fun times, and what they meant to us.

It is "more" because, as believers, the funeral for us was not only an occasion to celebrate Alli's life, but also a chance to encourage others of her life in Heaven and the life that *they* could have also.

Most unbelievers do not often think about eternity, and a funeral is one of those times when they do. In fact, I praise God that many people told us they really saw Jesus in the way we conducted ourselves during this time. I do not say this to boast, but as encouragement that Jesus can be reflected in our lives no matter what the situation.

As well, this very sad time was an opportunity for others to express themselves to us. We found being surrounded by people to be very important and helpful. I know not everyone would find this helpful, but for us this is what worked.

Most (if not all) people who want to express their compassion find that they do not know what to say or do when confronted with such a situation. People are going to say inappropriate things. I thank God that He gave me understanding to know how to deal with this. One way was to jump in and tell people before they had the chance to say anything that I knew they probably didn't know what to say. I told them this was to be expected because there really wasn't anything they *could* say to make the situation better. Honesty is always the way to go. Everybody I encountered seemed very relieved that I did that.

The second way was just to overlook those words which were intended to express compassion but weren't very helpful. I believe we can choose what we allow to plant in our hearts, and in such a vulnerable time as was this following a great loss, I believe that God protects His own. The inappropriate remarks will not generally take root in the grieving Christian's spirit.

Obviously, the people around us were just as devastated by Alli's death, and I found it helpful for them and for me to comfort and encourage *them*. I have always tried to see the needs of others and be of help, so I found that to be a natural thing for me to do. It gave me something to occupy my mind also. I knew people's hearts were full of love and compassion for us, and that was all I needed at the time. God's presence was so strong about me; I felt incredibly connected to and comforted by Him. It was a different story a few months down the road, however, but more on that later.

We decided (I think for ourselves as much as for the children) to have a private family burial a few days after the funeral. We didn't know how the kids would react, and we didn't want to overwhelm them (or ourselves!) any more than necessary. Some other details figured into the decision to wait not one, but three days. The day following the funeral was Mother's Day, and the day after that was Glori-Ann's birthday. We chose the third day, which was an absolutely beautiful May day. We believe we were simply taking care of her body; she wasn't there. To this day, the cemetery has no meaning for us. It holds no place of sadness, nor comfort, in our lives whatsoever.

It was quite a difficult thing for me to return to church the day after the funeral, especially on Mother's Day. After the funeral reception (which was held in our home), dear friends took the children for an overnight with their families from Saturday to Sunday. To remove the kids from the intensity of the funeral for a time was the best thing for them, but it didn't make Mother's Day any easier for me. I don't believe that anyone was really looking ahead to the next day and thinking about it being Mother's Day; the intent was to just give Oliver and me a little undisturbed time following the devastating events of the week.

On Sunday, the prevailing thought must have been to try to ignore the significance of the day, hopefully to help me get through it in one piece. That was a mistake. Significant days need to be significant. Being new to all this grief and loss, everyone tiptoed around me except for one neighbor. I saw him cutting his lawn and went over to talk to him. He wished me a happy Mother's Day. It was so sweet to be honored in spite of what had just happened in my life. Oliver and I came to understand that we couldn't overlook parts of everyday life and significant events because of losing Alli.

As for church, Oliver attended that morning to thank our church family for all their help and support. I stayed home. At that time there was no way in the world that I planned to set foot inside that church again. I wasn't rejecting Christianity or God or attending church; it was the physical place I found so disturbing.

In my mind, you see, Alli died at church. And that was true: She was actually physically killed just outside the church building. That Sunday evening, however, we as a family went to our church in the city we lived in before moving to Burlington. I don't know if I was thinking that maybe we would find another church to attend just by driving back and forth—in the past we had always sought the Lord when it came to decisions like that. At that point, I didn't have any great plans: I was still just taking life a few minutes at a time.

Again, I have to praise the Lord for His goodness and mercy and wisdom. During that Sunday evening service, the Lord gently spoke to me and told me that while it was true that Alli did die at the church, I didn't have to see it that way. He suggested that I see it as the place where Alli entered into His glory. After the Lord ministered that to me, the very next Sunday I was back in my usual seat at our church, praising the Lord.

5

The Aftermath

About two weeks after Alli died, we had a visit
from Family and Child Services. I thank God
that He prepared me for this somewhat as the
police officers involved in the case had fore-
warned me that the Services would be calling.
Apparently, a visit from them is a policy of some
sort when a young child dies.

Please understand that I am not making judgments on this government agency: I am simply
sharing what happened and how I was able to get
through it. There is no other way to characterize
it than to say it was an awful experience. I felt
completely under attack. It was so bad that after
the interview I almost felt like I couldn't even go
out and walk down the sidewalk without someone
coming to accuse me about the way I did it—if I
stepped in the wrong spot, I could be in big

trouble. In hindsight, what I experienced was the product of fear.

As you probably know, fear is the opposite of faith. It was still early on in this journey, but if I had allowed fear to continue to rule my heart and my mind, I would have, honestly, been unable to go on living.

I thank God that I was able to leave fear behind and operate in faith. During those first days following a tragedy, I saw how important it is to allow the presence of God surrounding you to propel you further into faith. It is much harder to get out of fear if that is all you allow in your heart and mind.

Even though we adjusted back into the routine of life after a couple of weeks, I was still some-what in shock and my thoughts raced all over the place. For the next four or five, possibly nine, months, I had weekly nightmares about other family members dying. Over time, those night-mares became less frequent. I hardly ever experience them now.

In this book I share with you many of the entries I made in a journal after Alli died. You may discover that you have had similar thoughts. It is important to realize that you are not alone in your experiences and that "normal" is a relative term.

May 31/01

My worst nightmare has come true. It still seems like a bad dream.

My baby! She was me entirely. [Of all of our children, Alli was absolutely me. All of the other kids took more after my husband, but Alli was so much like me. That was and is a hard thing to deal with.]

She was stolen from me.

I am so angry!

Alex always made the biggest messes. I'd give anything for one of her messes!

June 9/01
1 Month

How in the world can I possibly find pleasure in anything? It isn't fair! How can I enjoy myself doing some things knowing that had Alex not been killed, I wouldn't be doing it?

Will I ever start living again? Alex will never go to school. [The other children were school-aged, and Alex desperately wanted to go to school just like they did.]

June 19/01

Alex never got a chance to fulfill her purpose. Whenever it is mentioned that she has "gone home," it hurts because I still feel her home is here with me.... The phone calls and visits have stopped. So much tragedy happens every moment. We are a world of hurting people. Not only do we need God to heal our broken hearts; we need the power of God to stop the devil and his work. We need to move beyond healing and get to a place of living a divine life where the devil can't touch us. Prayer, fellowship, the Word...I am at a place where Jesus can't return soon enough...I want to see my precious baby! It still has not sunk in I don't think. Or maybe it has and I am being protected from overwhelming pain. I still want to know why, and I believe one day I can know and will know. Maybe that day will be today.

June 22/01

The kids have the reality that Alex was too young to die and that we need her. They want

Jesus to send her back. If only it were that easy and possible. I miss her. I am glad I was as expressive as I was with her. I know that she knew I loved her and liked her and enjoyed her. How I enjoyed her!

June 26/01

Driving down the highway, the tears just come. I can only hold it off so long…The pain builds and builds.

June 28/01

It seems Glori is in some ways trying to replace Alex. That's dangerous. She needs to be herself. I think all the stress is causing my hair to fall out. I've lost ten pounds. I feel like I should write a book. God has taught me so much, but at the same time, I don't have the answers to the questions I have. I want so much to be with the kids this summer, but I have to go back to work. That's the last thing I want to do. I can't stand not knowing if they are okay….

July 8/01

I've got the rest of my life to wonder whether I didn't love her enough to keep her on earth. If I stop grieving, if I stop missing her every second of every day, does that mean I didn't really love her enough? How do I reconcile not grieving for her and loving her so much?? I want to hold her in my arms!!

July 16/01

What I think the Lord has spoken to me...

—free will is the most important gift He's given man

—Alex didn't want to come back to earth after tasting Heaven; that's why she wasn't raised when the others spoke life into her.

—God can't and won't impose His will upon ours (including Alex)

—I will only know in part

—fight the devil from peace, not from anger

Will I ever know why the Lord didn't intervene and miraculously save her?

As you can see, my thoughts sometimes didn't flow in a logical pattern, but nonetheless, these were the things that ran through my mind. It helped me so much to acknowledge my thoughts, whether they were right and good or not so wonderful. I was then able to deal with a thought by either crying and praying through it, dismissing it as wrong or illogical, or just accepting it and moving on. At the end of the day, all our thoughts must be measured against the Word of God.

It's Later

As time went on, things got tough, especially in regard to exchanges with other people. As I have said, for a while after the funeral, the Spirit of the Lord was so heavy upon us, we appeared to be very strong and handling this tragedy well in spite of it all. As often occurs, appearances are deceiving.

About two weeks after Alli's death, I had an accident and separated my shoulder. It happened on a Saturday, but I was in church Sunday. I was in a lot of pain, on strong painkillers, but I was there. My arm was in a sling, so everyone at church soon knew what had happened (there were fewer than one hundred in the church at that time, membership having diminished following unrelated difficulties in the church six months before).

Even into August, two months after my accident, people came up to me at church to lovingly ask how my shoulder was. No one asked me anymore how my heart was. I had a huge problem dealing with that because Alli died outside that church, and no one could claim ignorance. I knew that, again, people didn't know whether they should bring up her death, and if they did, weren't sure of exactly what to say and didn't want to upset me. But I could not deal with people ignoring the "elephant in the room," so we started looking for a new church home. By the middle of October, we had found one and attend there to this day.

Oliver is so laid back, people's comments or lack of comments didn't bother him one way or the other. It just goes to show you, no two people are alike, even if they are married.

One Flesh, Two Souls

My husband and I, like most men and women, are very different in our approach to grief and our expression of it. Early on we agreed that although we were dealing with Alli's death differently, it was okay. We were not going to add to the already heavy load we were carrying as a family by expecting each other to react in a similar way.

To this day, Oliver and I don't talk very much about Alli's death. I think one of the keys to maintaining a positive marital relationship in the midst of such a tragedy is not only in focusing on the Lord, but also in respecting each other.

For example, there came a time (many times, in fact) when Oliver would share the details of exactly what happened when Alli went missing and everything that followed prior to my arrival. Although I knew the facts, I did not wish to hear them over and over again. I requested of my husband that he warn me he was about to discuss those things, and I would simply leave the conversation. Oliver, on the other hand, does not respond to grief in the way I do. He would rather not become overly emotional, so I try not to push him to express his feelings about Alli's death. Respect goes a long way.

Wives, submit yourselves unto your own husbands, as it is fit in the Lord. Husbands, love your wives, and be not bitter against them.

Colossians 3:18,19

6

Guilt, Blame — Warding Off Their Effects on Marriage

Families are extremely vulnerable when adversity such as the death of a child occurs. Very few studies have been done to determine how often the loss of a child leads to the divorce of the parents. In any case, the death of a child can lead to indifference, apathy, and emotional estrangement within the marriage.[1] That happened with me for a short time. Many people become lost in depression, which certainly doesn't help the situation. Marriage is hard work, and adversity such as this shakes the very foundation.

It has been commonly thought that 75% of the parents who lose a child eventually divorce. Actually, for parents to temporarily consider divorce is much more common and, even then, few actually carry through with the idea.

Feelings of guilt and assigning guilt, more than expressing blame, have a negative effect on a marriage. Either parent expressing guilt may also cause damage. Each parent should support the other in the other's expression of grief without taking it to such an extreme that they miss the common areas of response to grief they could be going through together.[2] After losing a child, a couple who knows the damage these conditions could cause to their marriage will know what to watch for and remain alert to ward them off.

You do not have to let the tragic loss hurt your marriage if you let a loving God take you through the experience. Actually, I believe that a tragedy can have the opposite effect; it can bring you and your spouse closer together as you deal with the overwhelming tribulation.

Thankfully, our family had built its foundation on the Solid Rock of Jesus Christ. The enemy had done his worst, but we were determined to stand together and not allow any more damage to be done to our family. Oliver and I avoided the "blame game" very intentionally.

Like every marriage, we had gone through the testing years and were at a place of peace and contentment in our marriage and family. I remember thinking a few days before Alli was killed that we were so blessed in our lives. Nothing tragic had ever happened to us. No one in our family had experienced any serious medical emergencies—no broken bones or anything else that might be considered a calamity.

Because Oliver was the one looking after the children that night, I know that many people expected me to place the blame on him. The truth is that blaming Oliver never crossed my mind. Later on, the more I thought about why I didn't blame him, the more I understood that it was for my own protection.

This realization was brought home to me one day when we were discussing our very different ways of grieving. I pressed Oliver to tell me why he didn't seem to express his feelings very much about Alli's death. I asked him because I wanted to understand. It was an extremely emotionally charged discussion, as you can imagine, and the type of discussion that I can remember having only twice.

When he started to share with me how he felt he should have heard the Holy Spirit clearer *before* she was killed, I stopped him immediately. I could not accept putting any of the blame on him because I believed that I could not remain in a relationship with him if I did. (At least, that was how I saw it.) Dissolving my relationship with him would have destroyed my life completely. I already felt that my life was pretty much in ruins as it was in the aftermath of Alli's death. That was the end of that!

I have come to understand that Oliver is, well, Oliver. Those who know him would know what I mean by this. It isn't that Oliver is shallow or uncaring, but he is very much an in-control, level-headed, logical kind of guy.

Oliver learned early on in his walk with the Lord that the Word of God is the measuring stick for all thoughts and actions. As such, not only did he decide that he would pour his time and energy into our remaining children, but he would take complete control of his thoughts and refuse to think on anything that was contrary to the truth of God's Word, and he is able to do this. I know that many faith believers work towards that, but for Oliver, that is an area where he has no problem. His refusal to dwell upon the accident and our loss was and is his spiritual survival.

The enemy, Satan, lies to us and tells us that if we do not dwell on our circumstances, we must not care about ourselves or the people around us who are also affected by those circumstances. Nothing could be further from the truth. The more we magnify our problems and circumstances, the less we can see God *in* those circumstances. Oliver understands this and walks in the truth. He felt no need to work through his emotions because he refused to give them place.

Myself, I found comfort and solace in talking to selected close friends whom I knew I could cry in front of without making them feel uncomfortable. Like most women, I work through my emotion in order to deal with it. Over time I realized that thoughts of Alli didn't consume my every waking moment anymore, and I came to understand that just because I didn't think about her 24/7 didn't mean that I loved her or missed her any less.

About three months after Alli's death, I received a call from the local Bereaved Families of Ontario office gently inquiring if they could be of service to my family and me. I was still somewhat under the blanket of the prayers of others in experiencing the protection of my emotions and sensing the close presence of God, and I saw this as an opportunity to help others. I thought since I had it all together (yeah, right!) maybe I could volunteer and help someone else who was going through grief. To become a volunteer, I first needed to attend at least one complete ten-week session of the program.

Although Bereaved Families of Ontario is not a church-sponsored program, bereavement some-times makes people more open to the Gospel. So off I went, ready to offer His comfort to those who were hurting and win the bereaved for Christ. Little did I know that I was about to be hit with reality.

Even though I was trusting in and leaning on the Lord, I was still grieving. It did help me to attend the grieving moms group. With a lot of tears shed, I came to see all kinds of ways that the Lord was working on my behalf throughout. Generally, women are social and communicative by nature and many find it helpful and healing to talk about what is going on in their lives. It helped me to be able to talk through my grief and read all I could about the things I was experiencing. It helped me to be reassured that the thoughts and feelings I was having were normal in order to be able to accept where I was and strive to reach where I wanted to be. I didn't have to stay in my grief any longer than necessary, and neither do you.

Church Leaders, Please Take Note

As a person in authority in the Body of Christ, a pastor and counselor have more expected of them, not only by God, but also by people in general. Authority in the Church has been put in place by God, and that is a good thing. In that respect, people, especially those grieving, look to the leadership for help and answers. In pointing out the huge need for helpful ministry for those who are bereaved, my intent is not to presume to judge anyone, but instead, to motivate leaders to give attention to learning how to support the bereaved in a way that will best minister.

Few Christians really know what to do with other Christians who have suffered a great loss. Obviously, it is important to lead a hurting person to Christ as a solution to their hurt. There also needs to be ministry available to help deal with all that follows a deep loss, the pain and questions, which don't automatically go away. Even though bereaved Christians know what the Bible says, especially in regard to the death of saved loved ones, dealing with and accepting the loss when it becomes a reality in your life isn't easy.

With as much training in ministry as Christians, especially those in leadership or counseling roles, unless they have lost a child or a spouse (it is sometimes different with a parent, because we are socialized to expect our parents to pass on in our lifetime), they really don't know what handling the loss is like. The bereaved need someone to understand what they are going through. I would encourage pastors, other types of leaders, or any other Christians to spend a little time studying the effects of loss and grief to give them some idea of what it is like. This understanding will help them know how to minister.

Even without a personal frame of reference, you can still be a loving and compassionate ear for those who have experienced loss and need you. The bereaved who have an understanding of the Word and a solid relationship with Christ, don't need teaching and preaching so much as a space to pour out their hearts without being judged or condemned for their wrong thoughts. They know the Word and have already judged and condemned themselves for their wrong thoughts and more!

There is a tendency among pastors, Christian counselors, and other Christians who have not experienced a great loss in ministering to those who have, to be quick to try to correct their process. Most of the time what the bereaved need is to verbalize their feelings in order to make sense of them and deal with them. They need your support more than you may think, no matter what it appears to look like on the outside.

Obviously, those who have experienced loss are generally the most helpful and understanding in ministering to others who have experienced loss. In my case, I have begun to step out and minister to others like me who have had to become members of a club they never wanted to join.

There is a family in our church whose son was recently killed by another person. Having been where they are, I am doing my best to stand alongside them to help support them as they adjust to life without their beloved son. I believe we all need to do what we can, every time we can. We have to be there for each other!

7

Letting Go and Letting God

There came a time shortly after Alli's death when I found myself in a situation which normally would have been enjoyable for me. But at the time, I felt like it would have been treason to be happy or laugh or have fun. I mean, what right did I have to experience pleasure when my daughter was dead?

Even though we in my family are Christians and believe with the eyes of faith that Alli is with God, it still took some time to accept the notion that she was alive in Heaven, not just dead on earth. For a couple months, I refused to accept her as being "home" with the Lord: her home was with me here on earth, not in Heaven. The time did come, however, when I was finally able to give her over to the care of the Lord. I remember the moment well.

As I was driving that night, I was wrestling with the Lord about Alli's death and had been for most of the way. But finally, with tears streaming down my face, I was able to let go and let Jesus have her. (By the way, I don't recommend doing that while driving: It is awfully hard to see through blinding tears!) Here is my journal entry about that experience:

> "Tonight I gave Alex back to the Lord. I have come to terms with her 'going home.' God is her Father and He entrusted me with her. I dedicated her to the Lord as an infant; it is time that I release her into His care. I'm going to have to release the other children. She is 100% safe;nothing can ever harm her. I will never ride on a train, ever! I hate trains!"

I want to share with you a revelation that someone gave me in regard to Alli being in Heaven. She is safe for all eternity now. We (Heaven forbid!) can possibly miss going to Heaven, but now that she has died, she is permanently saved: The devil can never have her! That revelation is so important to me as a parent. The salvation of our children is so vital, so important, and for me it is like, "One down, four to go." All of our children have an active, living relationship with the Lord, but one has already finished the course.

Adjusting to life without one of our precious daughters was and is not easy. Sometimes it is the little things that sneak up and send me spinning. I remember one evening when we went to a fast-food restaurant, I ordered six ice cream cones. It took me a minute to realize that I only needed five, not six. Another time I happened to see a little girl at church wearing a similar dress to the one Alli had worn the Christmas before she died. There is still the never-ending dilemma of whether I should tell people that I have four children or five. There are so many other little things like that that pop up; adjustment is an ongoing process.

Significant days are always an issue for grieving people. It helped me a lot that other people remembered Alli's birthday and also the day she died. That first Christmas, Krysti made me a picture frame with a drawing of Alli in it, and on the back she wrote, "I miss Alli too." I cried and cried! I tell you, that was so precious to me!

Every Christmas, we always took a photograph of the kids in front of the tree. When we got the film back of that first Christmas after Alli's death, it hit me hard to see the picture of just the three kids. (Zackary was still just a thought and possibility at that point!) I have a couple friends who never fail to remember Alli's birthday, and call me to see how I am doing. That means so much to me!

That first Christmas came and went; Alli's birthday came and went; the anniversary of her death came and went. As difficult as it was, those days didn't last forever. Time moves on. I don't quite know if I fully believe the adage "time heals all wounds," but I do know that God uses time to change one's perspective.

The Lord spoke to me early on in this journey and impressed upon my heart that my experience does not change God, but it does change me. He is the same yesterday, today and forever.[5] Just because I do not understand why something happened does not mean that it is God's character that is wrong. How I allow myself to be changed is, for a large part, mine to decide.

I chose to let God lead me through this. It was hard and it was painful, but I got through the worst of it. (I say "the worst of it" because you are never really completely "through" it, ever). I can't say that I did it right, because I messed up more times than I can count, but I did make it through into returning to a relatively normal activity-filled life, caring for my husband and children, and maintaining a strong relationship with the Lord—and am still making it through.

Sure, I still miss Alex so deeply that it hurts to think about it. Yes, I grieve sometimes at "what could have been but never will be," but it isn't the end of my world anymore. God is the Author of life, and there is still a lot of life I need to live and experience.

I can tell you with complete confidence and certainty now some years after Alexandra's death that only God can truly bring a person through such a trial. I honestly cannot imagine having to deal with this without the Lord to lean on. I also know that throughout the three short years we enjoyed Alli, neither Oliver nor I have any regrets about how we lived and loved her. May we all continue to have relationships with our children that leave us with no regrets!

Even though the day to day of life continued, my perspective was indeed changed in many respects. Problems still came at us but did not burden me down as they once did. The worst thing that could possibly happen to us has happened; we survived and came through it intact. After that, other problems are nothing we can't handle, and the little issues of life that crop up don't cause the same level of stress and anxiety as they once did. My faith wins over fear much more easily.

With each trial you go through and have victory over, the next one becomes a little bit easier. After all, trials are simply opportunities for victories of faith!

8

The Biggest Issue of All

At this point, I thought I was done telling my
story. But the Lord spoke again, so with tremen-
dous difficulty I continue to write. Perhaps the
hardest issue that this whole experience has
opened up is that of God's divine protection. I
was hoping to just gracefully ignore the issue. I
honestly don't think I have completely worked
through this dilemma, but I know that it may
indeed be the most important thing I deal with
on these pages (and certainly in my own life).

To reiterate an earlier point: We may never
have all the answers to all our questions in our life
on earth. I have thought of keeping a running list
of all the questions I want to ask the Lord when I
get to Heaven. Something like that may be
helpful. Even though I don't have the answer to
each question here, by writing it down I can rest

assured that I won't forget it and can consider it "taken care of" by God. Then I can stop thinking about it and get on with the business of living.

Although it is a good thing to learn from the past, we have to let go of it in order to live in the present and the future. We will only know in part, like the Bible says,[6] and that is something that we just have to accept. "I don't know" isn't the end of the world.

As I mentioned earlier, things were going well for us before Alli died. As you have probably experienced, we had our financial challenges, our times of needing to stand on the Word for good health, but I believed that we were somehow protected from any big disaster. After all, we were (and still are) children of God!

In working through this dilemma of divine protection; in retrospect, I saw some areas in my life to especially watch and attend to. I share them because of the importance to all Christians of remaining alert in maintaining them. Sometimes we gradually relax in some areas without realizing it and do it so gradually that we don't notice "the little foxes" that have come in to "spoil the vines."[7]

Divine Protection

I believe that Oliver and I simply took for granted the Lord's protection without actively possessing it. And therein lies the million-dollar question: How do you and I actively possess the divine protection (or anything else, for that matter) promised to us, which is from the Lord? Given the world events of the time in which we live, I think this is a particularly important issue to deal with.

I believe a part of faith is trusting or believing that God is in control. That doesn't mean that you or I have no choice or free will. We need to understand and believe in the Word of God and His covenant with us, and trust that He will keep His Word. As it relates to divine protection, the Lord is quite clear in His Word that we can expect Him to operate on our behalf.

Psalm 91

He that dwelleth in the secret place of the most High shall abide under the shadow of the Almighty. I will say of the LORD, He is my refuge and my fortress:my God; in him will I trust. Surely he shall deliver thee from the snare of the fowler, and from the noisome pestilence.He shall cover thee with his feathers, and under his wings shalt thou trust: his truth shall be thy shield and buckler.

Thou shalt not be afraid for the terror by night; nor for the arrow that flieth by day; Nor for the pestilence that walketh in darkness; nor for the destruction that wasteth at noonday. A thousand shall fall at thy side, and ten thousand at thy right hand; but it shall not come nigh thee. Only with thine eyes shalt thou behold and see the reward of the wicked. Because thou hast made the LORD, which is my refuge, even the most High, thy habitation; There shall no evil befall thee, neither shall any plague come nigh thy dwelling.

For he shall give his angels charge over thee, to keep thee in all thy ways. They shall bear thee up in their hands,lest thou dash thy foot against a stone. Thou shalt tread upon the lion and adder:the young lion and the dragon shalt thou trample under feet.

Because he hath set his love upon me, therefore will I deliver him:I will set him on high, because he hath known my name. He shall call upon me, and I will answer him: I will be with him in trouble; I will deliver him, and honour him. With long life will I satisfy him and shew him my salvation.

Psalm 91 is a much beloved portion of Scripture that shows us the promise of protection from the Almighty as do the following Scripture verses.

Wherefore ye shall do my statutes, and keep my judgments, and do them; and ye shall dwell in the land in safety.

Leviticus 25:18

For thou, Lord, wilt bless the righteous; with favour wilt thou compass him as with a shield.

Psalm 5:12

Every word of God is pure:he is a shield unto them that put their trust in him.

Proverbs 30:5

The God of my rock;in him will I trust:he is
my shield, and the horn of my salvation, my
high tower, and my refuge, my saviour; thou
savest me from violence.

2 Samuel 22:3

In the fear of the Lord is strong confidence:
and his children shall have a place of refuge.

Proverbs 14:26

Making It Real

It is very important to know what God says,
but how do we make it real in our lives? Thank
God, He tells us that, too.

And when Abram was ninety years old and
nine, the Lord appeared to Abram, and said
unto him, I am the Almighty God; walk
before me, and be thou perfect.

Genesis 17:1

"...*Be thou perfect....*" Well, that leaves me out
and, I suspect, you too. The thing is, we aren't
perfect in our walk as we follow God, and we all
make mistakes. But He has made provision for that.

Part of moving ahead is trusting in God's grace and mercy. We need to meditate upon Scripture related to God's goodness and love in order to realize again that we can trust Him and rely upon what He has done, what He is doing, and what He will still do for us. God is not the author of evil, and He truly hasn't caused evil to place you in your situation to teach you a lesson or anything like that.

> **Let no man say when he is tempted [enticed], I am tempted of God: for God cannot be tempted with evil, neither tempteth he any man.**
>
> **James 1:13 (addition mine)**

> **The thief cometh not, but for to steal, and to kill, and to destroy: I am come that they might have life, and that they might have it more abundantly.**
>
> **John 10:10**

But...

> **...For this purpose the Son of God was man-ifested, that he might destroy the works of the devil.**
>
> **1 John 3:8**

God really is on your side. He is always good and gives us good gifts, and He loves us very much.

O taste and see that the Lord is good:blessed is the man that trusteth in Him.

Psalm 34:8

Every good and perfect gift is from above, and cometh down from the Father of lights, with whom is no variableness,neither shadow of turning.

James 1:17

He that loveth not knoweth not God;for God is love.In this was manifested the love of God toward us, because that God sent his only begotten Son into the world, that we might live through him. Herein is love, not that we loved God, but that he loved us, and sent his Son to be the propitiation for our sins.

1 John 4:8-10

For God so loved the world, that he gave his only begotten Son, that whosoever believeth in him should not perish,but have everlasting life. For God sent not his Son into the world

to condemn the world; but that the world through him might be saved.

John 3:16,17

Perfect in Jesus— Even While Making Mistakes

Back to being "perfect": According to *Strong's Exhaustive Concordance of the Bible*, "perfect" in Genesis 17:1 means "without blemish, complete, full," ...sincere ("sincerely"), "sound, without spot, undefiled, upright," or "whole."[8] Right away in this definition I am reminded of the saving work of Jesus. The Word says that through Jesus, we have all been brought to a place of righteousness and perfection in God. What a relief! Yes, I make mistakes, but the righteousness and perfection of Jesus cover me!

There is a big "however" here—just because we are made perfect "in Christ" doesn't mean that we don't still have to make choices and decisions to walk and live according to the directions God has given us in the Bible. In the book of Romans, Paul addressed this very point.

What shall we say then? Shall we continue in sin, that grace may abound? God forbid. How shall we, that are dead to sin, live any longer therein? Know ye not, that so many of us as were baptized into Jesus Christ were baptized into his death? Therefore we are buried with him by baptism into death: that like as Christ was raised up from the dead by the glory of the Father, even so we also *should walk [AMP: live and behave] in newness of life.*

Romans 6:1-4 (emphasis mine)

Likewise reckon ye also yourselves to be dead indeed unto sin, but alive unto God through Jesus Christ our Lord.

Let not sin therefore reign in your mortal body, that ye should obey it in the lusts thereof. Neither yield ye your members as instruments of unrighteousness unto sin: but yield yourselves unto God, as those that are alive from the dead, and your members as instruments of righteousness unto God. For sin shall not have dominion over you: for ye are not under the law, but under grace.

What then? shall we sin, because we are not under the law, but under grace? God forbid. Know ye not, that to whom ye yield yourselves servants to obey, his servants ye are to whom ye obey; whether of sin unto death, or of obedience unto righteousness? But God be thanked, that ye were the servants of sin, but ye have obeyed from the heart that form of doctrine which was delivered you. *Being then made free from sin, ye became the servants of righteousness [amp: conformity to the divine will in thought, purpose, and action]* I speak after the manner of men because of the infirmity of your flesh: for as ye have yielded your members servants to uncleanness and to iniquity unto iniquity; even so now yield your members servants to righteousness unto holiness.

For when ye were the servants of sin, ye were free from righteousness. What fruit had ye then in those things whereof ye are now ashamed? for the end of those things is death. *But now being made free from sin, and become servants to God, ye have your fruit unto holiness, and the end everlasting life.* **For the wages of sin is death; but the gift of God is eternal life through Jesus Christ our Lord.**

Romans 6:11-23 (emphasis mine)

So we see that it is the will of God that we walk out our righteousness in agreement with our new life in Christ, giving sin no place, conforming to the divine will in thought, purpose, and action. Again, we won't do everything that we are supposed to do perfectly, but we need to do what we know to do and move on. Of course, to find out what God's will is we need to be reading and studying the Bible and praying, but we also need to *do* what the Bible says. That's action; being a doer of the Word, and not a hearer only.[9]

Ye shall walk after the LORD your God, and fear him, and keep his commandments, and obey his voice, and ye shall serve him, and cleave unto him.

Deuteronomy 13:4

And it shall come to pass, if thou shalt hearken diligently unto the voice of the LORD thy God, to observe and to do all his

commandments which I command thee this day, that the LORD thy God will set thee on high above all nations of the earth:

And all these blessings shall come on thee, and overtake thee, if thou shalt hearken unto the voice of the LORD thy God.

Deuteronomy 28:1,2

Cast not away therefore your confidence, which hath great recompence of reward. For ye have need of patience, that, after ye have done the will of God, ye might receive the promise.

Hebrews 10:35,36

And we desire that every one of you do shew the same diligence to the full assurance of hope unto the end: That ye be not slothful, but followers of them who through faith and patience inherit the promises.

Hebrews 6:11,12

My friend, the way you and I are going to possess the promises of God is through our obedience, patience, and faith in Him and His Word. As we actively conform our lives to the divine will of God by being a doer of the Word as wholeheartedly as we can, we will be blessed. And that blessing includes divine protection.

I read once that we as parents psychologically convince ourselves that we *can* protect our children, and when the "truth" (that we cannot) is exposed, it is quite devastating. It is true, we cannot be everywhere all of the time and control every possible situation, but I thank God that *because He is,* I don't have to be!

Even though outwardly life seemed smooth for my family, there were little foxes we had let come into our lives in the form of sins of disobedience that we just hadn't taken the time to deal with. These were things like not praying as we knew to or not reading the Word consistently, arguing over petty issues, not letting go of past mistakes, and bursting out with unforgiveness and bitterness we had allowed to build up. I do not for a second believe that somehow some secret deep, dark sin Oliver or I committed caused my precious daughter to be killed. But perhaps a pattern of little acts of disobedience did leave the door open for the devil to have access to our lives.

For the most part, I have simply ignored the implications of my own shortcomings as it may relate to Alli's death. I mean, how much pain can one person take?! Now the Lord is showing you His work on me in the hidden areas of my heart. My pain is your gain if somehow reading this helps you realize there are areas in your own life that need some loving divine attention.

The Still, Small Voice

Staying alert to listen for the Lord's voice, as distinct from His written Word, and being ready to obey it are other areas to consider. The Monday before Alli's death was the day that I was hired for the new job I started the evening of her death. When I was asked what day I could start, initially I felt that Thursday would be better. I could attend what would be my last midweek church service for the foreseeable future. I was asked if I could please come in Wednesday instead. I disregarded my feelings, my impression, and agreed to start Thursday.

In hindsight, I believe that the voice of God was directing me. I will never know definitively if recognizing that impression as His voice and hearkening to it was the one act that could have made the life or death difference, but it very well might have been.

You can imagine how that act of possible disobedience haunts me. The still, small voice[10] the Lord uses to speak to us can give us direction in what may seem to us an insignificant matter, yet be of disproportionately greater importance. We can never know what our obedience or disobedience to the Lord is going to result in at the time. But because the voice is small, it is also easy to ignore or not hear! We become heightened to recognizing the voice of the Lord by regularly spending time in His Word and communicating with Him in prayer.

My desire is for you to benefit from my experience and what I learned. But remember, we only know in part and may not know or ever know on earth the answer to the question, "Why?" We must guard against falling into a trap of guilt, blame, or living in the past.

Again, to remind you: Grief with its many thoughts and feelings is normal. You are not a wicked, backslidden person; you are grieving. Embrace the Healer of the broken hearted[11] and receive from Him. You will reach the turning point in your life in your own unique way, and you will move ahead with God.

9

The Test

One of the things Alli liked most was going to the park and playing on the swings. With four children, the park was a place where everyone could find something fun to do. After she died, it was perhaps the place I dreaded most. I summed it up in one of my journal entries:

July 3/01

I forget things so easily. Took the kids to the park. That is so hard for me...seeing all the kids playing. It's like my head is in a fishbowl. I can't help being overprotective. I miss my baby!

Of course, at ages three, five, seven, and nine, my children didn't go anywhere by themselves. There came a time the summer following Alli's death that my oldest son asked to go to one of the local parks with his friends *without* me. Boy, was that a huge request! I took a really deep breath and said okay, and off he went before I could change my mind. I had to continually fight fear to consciously *not* smother my children by being overprotective.

Not fifteen minutes had passed when there was a knock at the door. One of his friends had come to tell me that Jacob had fallen and hurt himself! Now Jake is a somewhat passionate and dramatic sort. Thinking he was overreacting, I told his friend to have Jake come home. His friend said, "No, you don't understand, he *really* hurt himself. He is bleeding everywhere and he can't walk!"

Thankfully, Oliver was home and jumped in the car to go get him. Jacob had sliced his leg open on a rock and needed stitches. So here I was, making my first real decision (after Alli died) to trust the Lord to keep my child safe, then disaster struck!

I had a very hard time not overreacting. In fact, I probably did overreact, but the children were patient with me knowing that I was trying to get a grip on being overprotective. The fact is, what happened to Jake was an accident, pure and simple. Stuff happens. The real test is in how we deal with it. I have learned that "how we deal with it" is subject to change over time, and the way we deal with that change is very important to our mental and emotional health.

During the weeks leading up to the fourth anniversary of Alli's death, I found myself extremely anxious and out of sorts. It took me about a week to figure out why I felt so agitated and disturbed. This was so different from the way I had coped in years past—I was confused by the way I was feeling.

Before, as a way of coping, I had always found being around people and talking about my experience to be helpful. This time, however, I wanted nothing to do with people; I didn't want to talk about it. I really didn't want to release a flood of heavy emotions either. I didn't have the energy. I asked the Lord about this change in my feelings. I believe He was showing me that people deal with negative things differently, especially if they do not know the Lord, and often people have to deal with both changing and negative emotions.

I was beginning to learn to listen to and obey the voice of the Lord more so than the desires of my flesh, and I felt giving in to the expression of my negative emotions in this case would have been acting in the flesh. Please understand, however, that I am not in any way equating expressing emotions with acting in the flesh. I certainly believe there is a time and place for expression of all emotions, and I have had my share of "expression." At that time in my life, however, I began learning to discern when negative emotions were appropriate, and this was not one of those times for me.

My experience showed me there are two main characteristics we need to have to be able to deal with negative emotions effectively: discernment and self-control. Discernment is necessary, not only in determining which emotions are simply negative and which are fleshly, but also in knowing what is safe to say and to whom.

Unfortunately, as time goes on, not everyone will understand your changing emotions. I am a staunch proponent of honesty, but not everyone will understand when you express having a bad day or a bad week or month. However well-intentioned they are, people who respond with, "It can't be that bad," or, "Well, tomorrow will be better," or, "I'm sure it is nothing," do not help. You have to be able to discern who the "safe" people are in your life and tailor your remarks accordingly. Sometimes that also takes self-control.

Exerting self-control is necessary to develop your walk in the Spirit.[12] It takes self-control not to give in to the desires of your flesh and exhibit carnal emotions. There is a difference between stuffing your negative emotions (by trying to ignore them, which is not helpful because they may resurface at inappropriate times) and casting them down according to the Word of God. Negative emotions need to be dealt with, but emotions that are of the flesh need to be cast down and let go of completely. No matter what you are dealing with, know that the Lord will continue to teach you the things you need in order for you to continue to grow and change.

When Really Big Stuff Happens Again!

Suddenly, everywhere I turned there seemed to be tragedy. When 9/11 happened, when the space shuttle Columbia blew up, and during the tsunami disaster of 2004, interestingly, my sorrow was more for the families going through the horror of losing someone dear to them. Separately from the sadness I felt for the people themselves who had been killed, I was overwhelmed with feelings of grief for the people who lost loved ones. Tragedy can change people: It certainly changed me! And for Christians, no matter how bad the loss was, although it seems unimaginable how God will turn it around for good at the time, "…we know that all things work together for good to them that love God, to them who are the called according to his purpose," as Romans 8:28 tells us.

I know the words of Jesus Christ are true:

These things I have spoken unto you,that in me ye might have peace.In the world, ye shall

have tribulation: but be of good cheer; I have overcome the world.

John 16:33

No matter who you are, you live in a world where bad things happen that just might affect your life. The way to survive them is to have the peace of God in your life. The Lord also says:

Come unto me, all ye that labour and are heavy laden, and I will give you rest. Take my yoke upon you, and learn of me; for I am meek and lowly in heart: and ye shall find rest unto your souls. For my yoke is easy, and my burden is light.

Matthew 11:28-30

Peace I leave with you, my peace I give unto you: not as the world giveth, give I unto you. Let not your heart be troubled, neither let it be afraid.

John 14:27

My friend, if you haven't already learned this, heart peace is found only in a relationship with Jesus and in a day-to-day active, living relationship with the Most High God. Jesus came to earth, died, was buried, and resurrected to provide the Way for us to have this relationship with God. The most wondrous thing about this is it is yours for the asking. Jesus died on the cross for *your* peace! All you have to do is receive Him, by faith, into your life.

This will not guarantee you a life free from troubles. In fact, troubles are almost guaranteed to come, but with Jesus as an active participant in your life, just as I do, you can know peace in the midst of dealing with the trouble that you need to walk through.

Throughout this journey, I have turned to the Word of God many, many times for inner strength, comfort, and peace. Below, I share with you several of the Scriptures that I not only searched out, but meditated on and prayed. Praying the Scriptures is a sure way to know that we are praying the right way, the way God teaches us in His Word, to bring results. God honors those prayers. The first passage that I remember meditating on is Isaiah 26:3-4 (AMP), which says:

You will guard him and keep him in perfect and constant peace whose mind [both its inclination and its character] is stayed on You, because he commits himself to You, leans on You, and hopes confidently in You. So trust in the Lord (commit yourself to Him, lean on Him, hope confidently in Him) forever; for the Lord God is an everlasting Rock [the Rock of Ages].

Praying Scripture aloud as opposed to just reading it actually does help. Faith comes by hearing the Word,[13] and praying aloud allows not only God, but also your own spirit to hear the petition of your heart. The prayer below is an example of how you can pray this particular Scripture.

Heavenly Father, I thank You for guarding me and keeping me in perfect and constant peace. I purposely commit my mind to thinking upon You. Lord, I am leaning on You and I rest my hope in You. I trust You, Lord, and I thank You that You are an everlasting Rock on which I can lean. Thank You for Your Word. In Jesus' name. Amen.

You can personalize and pray almost any portion of Scripture like this example. Other Scripture passages that ministered to me follow. You may want to personalize and pray many of them aloud yourself.

As other bereaved often do, I turned to the Book of Job. One passage that ministered to me was Job 13:3 (AMP):

> **Surely I wish to speak to the Almighty, and I desire to argue and reason my case with God [that He may explain the conflict between what I believe of Him and what I see of Him].**

This verse helped me immensely to understand there is a reason or explanation for what appeared to be the contradiction between who I believe God to be, what I see Him doing or not doing, and what my experience is.

Another Scripture that ministered to me is Psalm 34. It is a beautiful passage that speaks of protection, deliverance, and blessing.

Another one was Psalm 37. Verses 23-25:

The steps of a good man are ordered by the LORD: and he delighteth in his way. Though he fall, he shall not be utterly cast down: for the LORD upholdeth him with his hand. I have been young, and now am old; yet have I not seen the righteous forsaken, nor his seed begging bread.

I was knocked down, but the Word tells me I am neither cast down nor forsaken.

Psalm 93:4:

The LORD on high is mightier than the noise of many waters, yea, than the mighty waves of the sea.

Though the storm about me threatened to destroy me, the Lord is mightier!

Psalm 94:12-13 (AMP):

Blessed (happy, fortunate, to be envied) is the man whom You discipline and instruct, O Lord, and teach out of Your law, *that You may give him power to keep himself calm in the days of adversity,* **until the [inevitable] pit of corruption is dug for the wicked (emphasis mine).**

I am so glad for this Scripture! Throughout the funeral, burial, and the following weeks, I remained in a supernatural state of calm. In fact, I did not shed a tear at either the funeral or burial although I was very much in tune with what was going on. In *my* days of adversity, *I* was able to keep myself (well, I believe it was the Holy Spirit in me) calm.

For my thoughts are not your thoughts, neither are your ways my ways, saith the LORD. For as the heavens are higher than the earth, so are my ways higher than your ways, and my thoughts than your thoughts.

Isaiah 55:8,9

There is no getting around that one—He is God, and we are not! But we still have hope! Matthew 7:7 (AMP):

Keep on asking and it will be given you; keep on seeking and you will find; keep on knocking [reverently] and [the door] will be opened to you.

This is how I know that my questions can be answered some way, some day, some how. I have that hope. Mark 4:22 (AMP) backs that up:

> [Things are hidden temporarily only as a means to revelation.] For there is nothing hidden except to be revealed, nor is anything [temporarily] kept secret except in order that it may be made known.

One of the greatest comforts is found in 1 Thessalonians 4:13-18, a very common passage as it relates to the death of believing loved ones.

> But I would not have you to be ignorant, brethren, concerning them which are asleep, that ye sorrow not, even as others which have no hope. For if we believe that Jesus died and rose again, even so them also which sleep in Jesus will God bring with him.

> For this we say unto you by the word of the Lord, that we which are alive and remain unto the coming of the Lord shall not prevent them which are asleep. For the Lord himself shall descend from heaven with a shout, with the voice of the archangel, and with the

trump of God: and the dead in Christ shall rise first: Then we which are alive and remain shall be caught up together with them in the clouds, to meet the Lord in the air: and so shall we ever be with the Lord. Wherefore comfort one another with these words.

There are many, many more Scriptures that strengthen, encourage, and gird up the believer. If I listed them all—well—I would almost have to record the entire Bible. If you don't already do this regularly, please take the time to really read God's Word. It is a love letter written just for you no matter who you are, what you have done, what you are going through, or where you are in life.

Only God can take credit for healing my broken heart and giving me a new perspective and desire to keep on living, and I give Him all the glory. He is indeed the same yesterday, today, and forever. May you grow to know Him more and more, and may you stay close in your relationship with Him forever. If you don't know Him well, get to know Him. Believe in Him. Trust in Him. He cares for you!

Endnotes

Chapter 1

1 See John 10:10.

2 2 Corinthians 2:14.

Chapter 2

3 1 Thessalonians 4:13.

4 John 11:35.

Chapter 6

1 Mark Hardt Ph.D and Dannette Carroll, "http://www.healingheart.net/bereaved_parents_&_divorce1.htm" Bereavement Magazine, Sept/Oct 1999, 5125 N Union Blvd, Suite #4; Colorado Springs, CO 80918, "http://www.bereavementmag.com": See introductory paragraph.

2 Bereavement Magazine, Sept/Oct 1999.

Chapter 7

5 See Hebrews 13:8.

Chapter 8

6 1 Corinthians 13:9.

7 Song 2:15.

8 James Strong, "Hebrew and Chaldee Dictionary" in *Strong's Exhaustive Concordance of the Bible* (Nashville: Abingdon, 1890), p. 125, entry #8549, s.v. "perfect," Genesis 17:1.

Prayer of Salvation

God loves you—no matter who you are, no matter what your past. God loves you so much that He gave His one and only begotten Son for you. The Bible tells us that "…whoever believes in him shall not perish but have eternal life" (John 3:16 NIV). Jesus laid down His life and rose again so that we could spend eternity with Him in Heaven and experience His absolute best on earth. If you would like to receive Jesus into your life, say the following prayer out loud and mean it from your heart.

Heavenly Father, I come to You admitting that I am a sinner. Right now, I choose to turn away from sin, and I ask You to cleanse me of all unrighteousness. I believe that Your Son, Jesus, died on the cross to take away my sins. I also believe that He rose again from the dead so that I might be forgiven of my sins and made righteous through faith in Him. I call upon the name of Jesus Christ to be the Savior and Lord of my life. Jesus, I choose to follow You and ask that You fill me with the power of the Holy Spirit. I declare that right now I am a child of God. I am free from sin and full of the righteousness of God. I am saved in Jesus' name. Amen.

If you prayed this prayer to receive Jesus Christ as your Savior for the first time, please contact us on the Web at **www.harrisonhouse.com** to receive a free book.

Or you may write to us at:

Harrison House
P.O. Box 35035
Tulsa, Oklahoma 74153

About the Author

Pam Dressler makes her home in Hamilton, Ontario. She is currently attending McMaster University in Hamilton, pursuing a Bachelor of Arts in Sociology combined with a Bachelor of Social Work. Pam is an active member of Victory International Church located in Stoney Creek. This is her first published work, and

she is presently considering other writing projects with her husband, Oliver, a gifted storyteller. She is the mother of five children: Jacob, Krysti-Ann, Glori-Ann, Alexandra, and Zackary.

To contact Pam Dressler, e-mail her at:
findinghope@sympatico.ca

*Please include your prayer requests
and comments when you write.*

The Harrison House Vision

Proclaiming the truth and the power
Of the Gospel of Jesus Christ
With excellence;

Challenging Christians to
Live victoriously,
Grow spiritually,
Know God intimately.